From Bath With Love

From Bath With Love

An evocative view of Bath and the surrounding area by BOB CROXFORD

With an anthology compiled by Stella Pierce

"Let me counsel you not to waste your health in unprofitable sorrow,
but go to Bath and endeavour to prolong your life."

SAMUEL JOHNSON 1709-1784

Published by ATMOSPHERE

To Jenny & Becky,
Gavra & Naomi,
Good friends

FROM BATH WITH LOVE

Photographs copyright Bob Croxford 1995
Text copyright Bob Croxford 1995
(Except where separately acknowledged)

First published by ATMOSPHERE in 1995
Willis Vean
Mullion
Helston Cornwall TR12 7DF
TEL : 01326-240180
FAX : 01326-240900

ISBN 0 9521850 2 4

Designed by Ann Butcher
Origination by Scantec, Falmouth
Printed and bound in Italy by IPF - Maniago / PN

Also by BOB CROXFORD

FROM CORNWALL WITH LOVE	*ISBN 09521850 0 8*
FROM DEVON WITH LOVE	*ISBN 09521850 1 6*
FROM THE COTSWOLDS WITH LOVE	*ISBN 0951850 4 0*
FROM DORSET WITH LOVE	*ISBN 09521850 3 2*
HAMPSHIRE	*ISBN 09521850 5 9*
A VIEW OF AVALON	*ISBN 09521850 6 7*
THE CORNISH COAST	*ISBN 09521850 7 5*

COVER PICTURE : The Royal Crescent

CONTENTS

INTRODUCTION

Dawn. The overnight mist lies low and thick in the Avon valley. At Bradford-on-Avon it clings heavy and damp. The dew-fall in the water meadows creates strings of crystal pearls on spiders' webs. The mist at Bath lifts and drifts down river towards Bristol.

The first rays of the sun reflect red on the windows of homes perched on the hills above Bath. In Victoria Park, fire roars like a dragon, as a hot-air balloon lifts into the still air. Champagne corks pop aloft.

Down below the sleeping city stirs. The milkman's van rattles on the cobblestones of The Royal Crescent. A postman cycles round Laura Place. A dust-cart bangs its way round Queen Square. A newsboy pushes the morning papers through letter-boxes on Lansdown Crescent. Office cleaners let themselves into old buildings which once were scenes of all night gambling parties, but which now house sober solicitors. The bakers, in pastry shops across town, warm their ovens to bake a variety of breads, brioches and cakes.

The city slowly wakes. Early morning tea for Japanese and American tourists in luxury hotels. The school run, for a harassed mum, in a beat-up Volvo. Rush hour traffic jams as workers who live in Bristol, but work in Bath, pass those who live in Bath and work in Bristol!

Shopkeepers open their doors. The Pump Room staff, weary-eyed after a party the night before, prepare to serve the first coffee of the day. A small queue forms at the entrance of the Roman Baths. The doors open. Bath is ready for business once more.

Every day of the year for the past sixteen centuries the City of Bath has played host to visitors while working away at its own trades. Weavers worked side by side with the sick, who came to take the waters. While Romans spent money the Bath Mint made more. Now computer programmers and graphic designers work where Georgian Society gossiped.

Bath is a City which needs approaching in the correct frame of mind. Arrive in the rush hour in the middle of summer, battle to find a parking place, walk through crowded streets to find standing-room only pubs and cafes, is the wrong way. Arrive at dawn to find the town deserted, the sun creating dramatic reliefs on mellow stone, sit and admire the view and observe the city coming to life, and you'll feel good all day.

I first fleetingly visited Bath in my late teens and again in the 1960s. It has changed a lot in 35 years. The buildings, which now shine so magnificent in the sun were once black. Two or more centuries of soot from coal fires made them dark and sombre.

Traffic has always been a hazard. In Georgian times the hazard was horse manure. Ladies in long dresses would ride in sedan chairs, not out of idleness but, to keep their clothes clean. To cross the road often required a tip to a man with a broom who cleared a temporary pathway through the muck. Now the hazard is the motor car.

This book of photographs is a collection of portfolios, The Baths, Floral Bath, The River, etc. My view is that of an individual. This is what it looked like at the moment of pressing the shutter. I have not altered or distorted the scene. If you lie down on the grass, as many do in midsummer, The Royal Crescent really does look like the cover. A stroll in early morning or late afternoon, when the sun glances revealingly on old facades, reveals time-worn and timeless vistas.

BOB CROXFORD

It is a morbid thought to contemplate whether some day the volcano below Bath may change its mind about sending up water and deliver a charge of explosive gasses and lava. It has behaved itself for centuries so I suppose there is no good reason why it should not go on behaving itself. Volcanoes have, no doubt, their own code of behaviour.

VICTOR CANNING 1936

Where the hot springs, circulating in channels beneath the surface, are conducted by channels artificially constructed, and are connected into an arched reservoir, to supply the warm baths which stand in the middle of the place, most delightful to see and beneficial to health; ... infirm people resort to it from all parts of England, for the purpose of washing themselves in these salubrious waters; and persons in health also assemble there, to see the curious bubbling up of the warm springs, and to use the baths.

HENRY OF HUNTINGTON 12th Cent.

◀ *Gorgon's Head*
Hot Spring Overflow ▶

*A*gricola arrived in the middle of summer in the year of Rome 831. In order, by a taste of pleasures, to reclaim the natives from that rude and unsettled state which prompted them to war, and reconcile them, to quiet and tranquillity, he incited them, by private instigations and public encouragements, to erect temples, courts of justice, and dwelling-houses.

He was also attentive to provide a liberal education for the sons of their chieftains, and his attempts were attended with such success, that they who lately disdained to make use of the Roman language, were now ambitious of becoming eloquent. Hence the Roman habit began to be held in honour, and the toga was frequently worn. At length they gradually deviated into a taste for those luxuries which stimulate to vice; porticos, and baths, and the elegancies of the table: and this, from their inexperience, they termed politeness, whilst, in reality, it constituted a part of their slavery.

CORNELIUS TACITUS AD 80

..the Baths were like so many Bear Gardens, and Modesty was entirely shut out of them; People of both Sexes bathing by Day and Night naked; and Dogs, Cats, Pigs and even human Creatures were hurl'd over the Rails into the Water, while People were bathing in it.

JOHN WOOD The Elder 1704-1754

This bath is the moſt frequented by the quality of both ſexes, where, with the greateſt order and decency, the gentlemen keep to one ſide of the bath, and the ladies to the other. No gentleman whatever muſt preſume to bathe in the ladies' diſtrict, under a pecuniary mulct, inflicted by the ſerjeants of the bath: the ladies are ſuppoſed to be ſo modeſt as not to come near the gentlemen.

SAMUEL GALE 1705

*S*trict injunction and order to the archdeacon of Bath and his offi-cial, and all the rectors, vicars and chaplains of the city and archdeaconary of Bath, - on a report which has reached the ears of the bishop that the heavenly gift of warm and healing waters with which the city of Bath has been endowed from of old is turned into an abuse by the shamelessness and uncleanness of the people of that city, insomuch that, when any persons, whether male or female, go to the said waters to bathe and recover their health, and through modesty and shame try to cover their privy parts, the men with drawers (femoralibus) and the women with smocks (subunculis), they, the said people, by what they say is established custom of the city, barbarously and shamelessly strip them of their said garments and reveal them to the gaze of the bystanders, and inflict on them not only the loss of their garments but a heavy monetary fine,- during mass on Sundays, solemn days and feast days, to admonish all the citizens of Bath, and all others staying there, that they abstain from such excesses under penalty of the greater excommunication, and to enjoin on them, under a like penalty, that henceforth no males or females who have reached puberty go to the baths without wearing such drawers and smocks or other linen garments.

BANWELL   29th August 1449

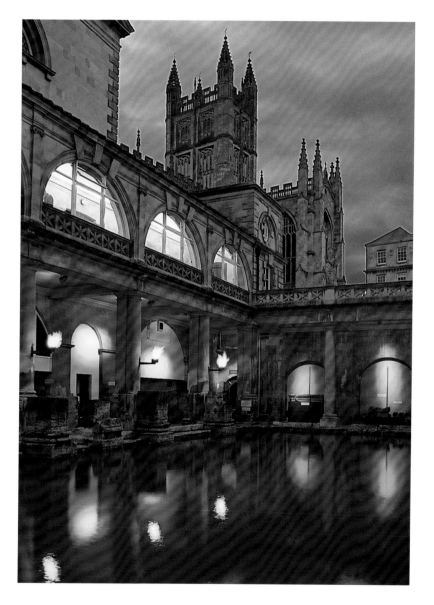

Re: the statue of Bladud in the baths

*B*ut I have likewise another embassey to your Majesty; this is from King Bladud, who (as the Bath Guide informs us) reigned in England about 900 years before Christ, and was the first discoverer of these springs. This King keeps his state on a fine rotten post in the middle of the water, decorated with a long account of his pedigree. His Majesty whispered me the other day that having heard of your fame, he has long wished to see you, he says that, except his sister of Orange, he has not seen a royal female for a long time; and bid me at the same time assure your majesty, that tho' in his youth, about three thousand years ago, he was reckoned a man of Gallantry, yet he now never offers to take the least advantage of any lady bathing beneath his Throne, nor need the purest modesty be offended at his glances.

RICHARD BRINSLEY SHERIDAN 1751-1816

"Have you drank the waters, Mr. Weller?" inquired his companion, as they walked towards High Street.

"Once," replied Sam.

"What did you think of 'em, sir?"

"I thought they wos particklery unpleasant," replied Sam.

"Ah," said Mr. John Smauker, *"You disliked the killibeate taste, perhaps?"*

"I don't know much about that 'ere," said Sam. *"I thought they'd a wery strong flavour o' warm flat-irons."*

"That is the killibeate, Mr Weller," observed Mr. John Smauker, contemptuously.

CHARLES DICKENS 1880

BILL OF FARE

FIRST COURSE

Turtle, with Punch a la Romaine.
Turbot and Lobster sauce and Cod and Oyster Sauce.
Stewed and Fried Fish
Roast Beef. Rump of Beef. Haunches & Saddles of Mutton.
Roast & Boiled Turkeys. Hams & Tongues. Boiled Chickens.
Ornamented Savoy Cakes.
Fillets Pork, and Tomato Sauce. Palates de Boeuf.
Sweetbreads a la Bechemelle, with Truffles.
Fillets de Mouton, Sauce a la Soubise. Veal Tendrons,
Chicken and Ham Rissoles. Lobster and Oyster Patties.
Pyramids of Ornamented Pastry.

SECOND COURSE

Pheasants. Hares Partridges. Woodcocks.
Snipes. Wild Ducks. Teal.
Cabinet Pudding. Mince Pies
Ramequins a la Sefton
Apple & Damson Tarts, Plum Puddings.
Variegated Jelly a la Victoria.
Neapolitan Cake. Macaroni au Gratin.
Lobster Salads
Vanilla Cream, and Creams Varied.
Orange Jelly.
Stilton Cheese. White Cheddar. Butters.
Salads. Lobsters.

DESSERT

Pines. Grapes. Apples. Pears. Walnuts. Medlars.
Muscatels and Almonds. Oranges. Savoy Cakes.
Almond Cakes. Fancy Biscuits.

ANON 18TH DECEMBER 1850

We all went to see Bathe where I bathed in the Crosse Bathe. Amongst the rest of the idle diversions of the toune one musitian was famous for acting a changeling, which indeede he personated strangley. The faciate of this cathedrall is remarkable for its historical carving. The King's Bathe is esteem'd ye fairest in Europe. The toune is entirely built of stone, but the streetes narrow uneven and unpleasant.

EVELYN June 27 1654

I like Bath: it has quality. I like Bath buns, Bath Olivers, Bath chaps, Bath brick, and Bath stone (which to my London eyes is the beautiful sister of Portland stone), and few sights are more stimulating to relaxed nerves than to sit on the hotel terrace opposite the Pump Room and watch the Bath chairs dash past.

H V MORTON 1927

◀ *Statue of Beau Nash*
The Pump Room ▶

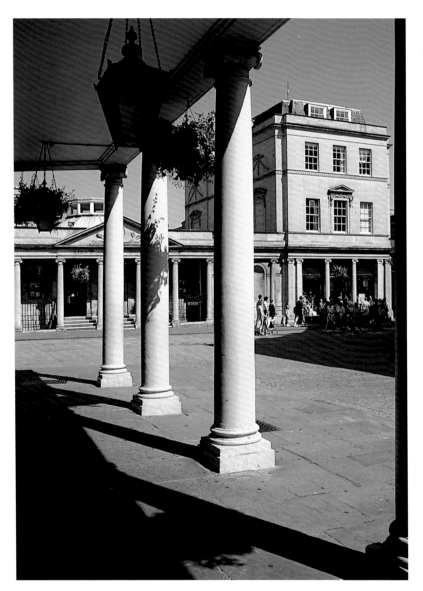

Sat - Up at 4 a'clock being by appointment called up to the (Cross) Bath where we were carried after one another myself and wife and Betty Turner Willett and WH. And by and by though we designed to have done before company came-much company came-very fine ladies and the manner pretty enough only methinks it cannot be clean to go so many bodies together in to the same water. Good conversation a among them that are acquainted here and stay together. Strange to see how hot the water is and in some places though this is the most temperate bath the springs so hot as the feet not to endure. But strange to see what women and men herein that live all season in these waters that cannot but be parboiled and look like the creatures of the Bath. Carried back wrap in a sheet and in a chair home and there one after another thus carried (I staying above two hours in the water) home to bed sweating for an hour and by and by comes music to play to me extraordinary good as ever I ever I heard at Landon almost any where.

SAMUEL PEPYS 13th June 1668

◀ *The Collonades*
Cross Street Baths ▶

*T*hey determined on walking round Beechen Cliff, that noble hill, whose beautiful verdure and hanging coppice render it so striking an object from almost every opening in Bath.

"I never look at it," said Catherine, as they walked along the side of the river, "without thinking of the south of France."

JANE AUSTEN 1897

*W*henever I go to Bath I always make my pilgrimage to the tip of Beechen Cliff. There is no greater joy than to look down upon the city through the still air of a bright morning. The last time I saw it was on a morning when there was just enough haze to enhance its beauty without blurring its outlines. Framed in the firs and beeches of the cliff-top it lay quietly in the valley-bottom surrounded by guardian hills, its grey-brown houses and streets spreading up the sides of a natural bowl, a city of incomparable grace and precision, the creation of orderly and beauty-loving minds.

VICTOR CANNING 1936

*B*ath is sette booth yn a fruteful and pleasant botom which is invironed on every side with great walls out of which cum many springes of pure water that be conveyid by dyverse ways to serve the Cyte. There be four gate yn the town by the names of Est, etc. The waulle within the town is of no great height to the eyes, but without it is a fundamentis of reasonable heighth: and it standith allmoste alle, lakking but a peace about "Gascoyne tower". This took its name from one Gascoyne, who in hominum memoria built a peace of walle as amends for a fault committed in the city.

LELAND c1540

*T*he very fact that the delightful place or scene was discovered by us made it the shining place it is in memory. Again, the charm we found in it may have been in a measure due to the mood we were in, or to the peculiar aspect in which it came before us at the first, due to the season, to atmospheric and sunlight effects, to some human interest, or to a conjunction of several favourable circumstances; we know we can never see it again in that aspect and with that precise feeling.

On this account I am shy of revisiting the places where I have experienced the keenest delight.

W H HUDSON 1909

Gabriel's features seemed to get thinner. "Well, what did you see besides?" "Oh, all sorts." "Well, what besides?" "Great glass windows to the shops, and great clouds in the sky, full of rain, and old wooden trees in the country round." "You stun-poll! What will ye say next?" said Coggan. "Let en alone," interposed Joseph Poorgrass. "The boy's maning is that the sky and the earth in the Kingdom of Bath is not altogether different from ours here. 'Tis for our good to gain knowledge of strange cities, and as such the boy's words should be suffered, so to speak it." "And the people of Bath," continued Cain, "never need to light their fires except as a luxury, for the water springs up out of the earth ready boiled for use." "'Tis true as the light," testified Matthew Moon. "I've hear other navigators say the same thing." "They drink nothing else there," said Cain, "and seem to enjoy it, to see how they swaller it down." "Well, it seems a barbarian practice enough to us, but I daresay the natives think nothing o' it," said Matthew. "And don't victuals spring up as well as drink?" asked Coggan, twirling his eye. "No - I own to a blot there in Bath - a true blot. God didn't provide 'em with victuals as well as drink, and 'twas a drawback I couldn't get over at all." "Well, 'tis a curious place, to say the least," observed Moon; "and it must be a curious people that live therein."

THOMAS HARDY 1874

In such a narrow Compassis this antient, famous, little, pretty City contained, which being in such a Bottom, had such a Variety of Prospects and Landskips, that few Places parallel it.

H C CHAPMAN 1631

Towns may be divided, if you care for that peculiar pleasure, into certain types. There are, of course, the towns we are born in, the towns we visit and leave as soon as possible never to return again, the towns we visit and return to as often as we can the towns we work in, and the towns in which we would like to have been born.

Apart from Bath I know of no town which, for myself I can promote to the last class. Had I any say in the circumstances of my birth, and had I been granted a pre-natal knowledge of this country, I should have said politely, yet firmly : " If it is all the same to everybody concerned I should like to be born in Bath."

VICTOR CANNING 1936

Certainly Bath seems to be a place favourable to longevity; it reminds me of those tranquil ponds in which carps, forgotten by the angler, live to a fabulous age... Its mild and misty melancholy gains upon one and engenders a languid affection.... If I come to Bristol I will certainly pay my respects to your Ladyship, but at present I have fallen into the carp-like state of meditative laziness, and my excursions are limited to a slow swim up and down the pond.

LORD LYTTON 1803 - 1873

*H*ere a good Organ but a vain pragmatic fellow preached a ridiculous sermon affected that made me angry and some gent that sat next to me and sang well. So home walking round the walls of the city which are good and the battlemts all whole.

So home to dinner.

June 14th and after dinner comes Mr. Butts again to see me and he and I to church where the same idle fellow preached. And I slept most of the sermon. Thence home and took my wife out and the girls and came to this church again to see it and look over the monuments where among others Dr Venner and Pelling and a lady of Sr W Wallers he lying with his face broken.

SAMUEL PEPYS 14th June 1668

*T*hese walls adorned with monument and bust
Show how Bath Waters serve to lay the dust

HENRY HARRINGTON 1727-1816

My dear Temple,   Bath, Sunday, 28th April 1776.

I am now, for the first time, at this most elegant city, which far
exceeds my expectations. I will not attempt a description of it. I have
no pencil for visible objects. I can only paint the varieties of mind,
of l'esprit. You who gave me so good a picture of Mount Edgecumbe
could also describe Bath; and what would I give to have you here!
It is the finest place on earth for you; for you may enjoy it's society
and it's walks without effort or fatigue.

JAMES BOSWELL

THE CERTIFICATES already issued for wearing HAIR-POWDER
will expire on the 5th day of April.
Persons wearing Hair-Powder after the 5th of April, who have not
taken out Certificates, will incur the Penalty of TWENTY POUNDS
on information and conviction, before a Justice of the Peace. One
half of the Penalty goes to the person making the information.

BATH JOURNAL 1st May 1797

*T*hey arrived at Bath. Catherine was all eager
   delight; - her eyes were here, there,
everywhere, as they approached its fine and
striking environs, and afterwards drove through
those streets which conducted them to the hotel.
She was come to be happy, and felt happy
already.

They were soon settled in comfortable lodgings in
Pulteney Street.

JANE AUSTEN 1897

*D*uring the winter season of Bath in the latter part of the year
   1778, or the beginning of 1779, two of its visitors were
Count Rice and Viscount du Barre, who coming from the German
Spa, resided in the same house for some weeks at Bath, but an unfortunate quarrel arising, partly of a domestic nature; the impetuous
disposition of du Barre determined the dispute should terminate with
the non-existance of one of them, and with that madness of despera-
tion they left the Three Tuns Inn, in Stall-street, provided with
arms, seconds, and surgical assistance; long before the rising of the
sun, they had traversed in a chaise, the Downs of Claverton and
Hampton, waiting for the approach of day; at length the dawn
began to break, the distance was measured, and Count Rice fired
first without affect: du Barre returned the fire, and the ball lodging
in the groin of his antagonist, he fell; but raising himself from the
ground he discharged the second pistol, the contents of which pene-
trated the heart of the unfortunate du Barre, he was buried in the
church yard of Bath-Hampton, where a stone discribes the spot of his
interment; Count Rice was tried at Taunton, at the Lent assizes,
1779, and acquitted.

ANON 1813

*O*f all the towns in the Kingdom Bath is the most extraordinary, not to say ridiculous in its topographical and street nomenclature. Of course we understand all its "Ups" being "Downs" (that is a general eccentricity in the south of England), and one of its lowest thoroughfares, "High St.," but it is slightly bewildering to find one of its narrowest streets "Broad Street", its "North Road" leading due south. The only appropriately named district of Bath is the Dolemeads. Trim-street is not particularly trim, Cheap-street is not particularly cheap, nor is Green Street very green, while Old Bond Street is not a street at all.

M J B BADDELEY 1908

*J*anuary 8 - We arrived at Bath last night. The chaise drew up in style at the White Hart. Two well-dressed footmen were ready to help us to alight, presenting an arm on each side. Then a loud bell on the stairs, and lights carried before us to an elegantly furnished sitting-room, where the fire was already blazing. In a few minutes, a neat-looking chambermaid, with an ample white apron pinned behind, came to offer her services to the ladies, and shew the bed-rooms. In less than half an hour, five powdered gentlemen burst into the room with three dishes, &c. and two remained to wait. I give this as a sample of the best, or rather of the finest inns.

LOUIS SIMON 1816

To-day I passed through Lilliput Alley where Sally Lun kept her cake-shop.

No more I heed the muffin's zest,
The Yorkshire cake or bun;
Sweet muse of pastry: teach me how
To make a Sally Lun.

HORACE ANNESLEY VACHELL 1933

*T*hese Bath-buns are almost the same preparation as the Brioche cakes so much eaten and talked of in Paris.

MARGARET DODS 1826

"*A* solitary porter shuffles along the platform. Yonder, those are the lights of the refreshment room, where all night long, a barmaid is keeping her lonely vigil over the beer-handles and the Bath buns in glass cases."

MAX BEERBOHM 1923

AN Act of Parliment paffed in the thirtieth Year of the Reign of his late Majefty King George the Second, inflicts the Penalty of Twenty Shillings on every Journeyman, Labourer, Servant or Apprentice, playing at any Ale-Houfe with Cards, Dice, Draughts, Shuffle-Boards, Miffiffippi, or Billard-Tables, Skittles, Nine-Pins, or with any other Implement of Gambling.

STATE LOTTERY

TICKETS, Shares and Chances, are now felling in great Variety, and at the loweft Prices, by WILLIAM and ROBERT CLEMENT, Linen-Drapers, in Wade's-Paffage, Bath; Where all Bufinefs concerning Lotteries is tranfacted with Punctuality. Begins drawing next Monday fe'nnight, fo there's no Time to be loft.

N.B. We fell Bombazines, Norwich Crapes, Poplins, and various Kinds of Stuffs for Mourning, as alfo fuperfine Long-Lawns and Muflins of all Breadths.

BATH CHRONICLE 7th November 1765

I n the city and borough of Bath, while there are 74 bakers shops, 51 butchers shops, there are within the same area 300 places for the sale of intoxicating drinks - not just for public convenience but in many instances are the haunts of the idle and dissipated to the serious injury of public morals.

ANON 1867

One of the wonders of the journey was a warm-water spring on the outskirts of Bath, which was crowded with people. The greenery of Bath resembles Mazanderan; the houses are built of white stone.

I asked Mr. Morier about the throng of people and he explained that the spring is a manifestation of the power of Almighty Providence. Around it are built baths of various sizes and water is brought from it to them in stone conduits. The spring waters are endowed with special curative properties and the people we saw were invalids brought from all over England. Some are made to drink the waters; others to bathe in them. Then, God willing, they are cured.

After visiting the spring and the baths, we drove towards the city. A wide river flows through the middle of the town and over the river is a sturdy bridge. The streets are well laid out with houses and many churches, of differing design, but all built of white stone. Small rivulets flow down both sides of the street. The city is as beautiful as a flower-garden and the visit delighted me.

MIRZA ABUL HASSAN KHAN 1809

Peace hath here found harbourage mild as every sleep:
Not the hills and waters, the fields and wildwood bowers,
Smile or speak more tenderly, clothed with peace more deep,
Here than memory whispers of days our memories keep
Fast with love and laughter and dreams of withered hours.
City lulled asleep by the chime of passing years,
Sweeter smiles thy rest than the radiance round thy peers;
Only love and lovely remembrance here have place
Time on thee lies lighter than music on men's ears
Dawn and noon and sunset are one before thy face.

ALGERNON CHARLES SWINBURNE 1905

The Bathonians have a new Theatre for plays; over the door is this inscription in golden letters,

PLAYS ARE LIKE MIRRORS, MADE FOR MEN TO SEE,
HOW BAD THEY ARE, HOW GOOD THEY OUGHT TO BE.

SAMUEL GALE ESQ. 1705

First then, out of zeal for your Majesty, I cannot forbear informing you that the said Society have come to a resolution to address your Majesty to dissolve your court in Soho, and adjorn to Bath: this they humbly conceive will be much to the benefit of your Majesty's health, and spirits; the latter of which they know you stand particularly in need of:

RICHARD BRINSLEY SHERIDAN 1751-1816

It had been a frosty morning, to be sure, a sharp frost, which hardly one woman in a thousand could stand the test of. But still, there certainly were a dreadful multitude of ugly women in Bath; and as for the men! they were infinitely worse. Such scarecrows as the streets were full of! It was evident how little the women were used to the sight of anything tolerable, by the effect which a man of decent appearance produced.

JANE AUSTEN 1897

"What takes you to Bath, Sherry?"
"My mother. She's putting up at Grillon's with the Incomparable. Both going to Bath to drink the waters. I'm to escort 'em."
Ferdy gazed at him in dismay. "I wouldn't do it, Sherry," he said. "You won't like it there!"
"Well, if I don't like it, I can come back, can't I?"
"Much better not go at all, " said Ferdy. "Very dull sort of a place these days. Don't even waltz there. Won't like the waters either."
"Good God, I ain't going to drink 'em!"

GEORGETTE HEYER 1944

◀ *Abbey Green*
Shire's Yard ▶

THE NEWEST BATH GUIDE

Off all the gay places the world can afford,
By gentle and simple pastime ador'd,
Fine balls, and fine concerts, fine buildings, and springs,
Fine walks, and fine views, and a thousand fine things,
(Not to mention the sweet situation and air,)
What place, my dear mother, with Bath can compare?

CHRISTOPHER ANSTEY : THE NEW BATH GUIDE, 1766

It is two hundred years since he got in his stride
And Cantered away with The New Bath Guide.
His spondees and dactyls had quite a success,
And sev'ral editions were called from the press.
That guidebook consisted of letters in rhyme
On the follies and fashions of Bath at the time:
I notice a quiver come over my pen
As I think of the follies and fashions since then....

Proud City of Bath with your crescents and squares,
Your hoary old Abbey and playbills and chairs,
Your plentiful chapels where preachers would preach
(And a different doctrine expounded in each),
Your gallant assemblies where squires took their daughters,
Your medicinal springs where there wives took the waters,
The terraces trim and the comely young wenches,
The cobbled back streets with their privies and stenches-
How varied and human did Bath then appear
As the roar of the Avon rolled up from the weir.

In those days, no doubt, there was not so much taste:
But now there's so much it has all run to waste
In working out methods of cutting down cost-
So that mouldings, proportion and texture are lost
In a uniform nothingness. (This I first find
In the terrible "Tech" with its pointed behind.)
Now houses are "units" and people are digits,
And Bath has been planned into quarters for midgets.
Official designs are aggressively neuter,
The Puritan work of an eyeless computer.

Goodbye to old Bath! We who loved you are sorry
They're carting you off by developer's lorry.

JOHN BETJEMAN

◀ *Untaxed Window*
Queen Square House ▶

After a month's convalescence, his fell disease subsided, he felt "almost like a human being again" and well enough to go off for "a perfect week-end with Roger' to Bath. They stayed together at the Pulteney Hotel, in Laura Place -"a perfect spot - and quite a sympathetic establishment," he told Carrington, 'with a lift boy no less sympathetic, who at last said to me (in a broad West Country accent) "Excuse me, zurr, bout are you the zelebrated author?"... We inspected all the favourite sights - including Prof. Saintsbury at No.1 the Crescent - his white hair and skull-cap were visible as usual through the window.

LYTTON STRACHEY 1929

He stared at Leonard, then glanced up at the red light. The light was about to change when the man asked Leonard if he knew where the Royal Crescent was. The man's arms were scrawny. So was his voice. Mid-Western. Maybe Arkansas. They were both wearing powder blue and the man a white cotton cap. Leonard was surprised they did not know Royal Crescent. He assumed that was the sort of thing Americans would know, instinctively. It took some explaining. They produced a tourist map. She pointed to the grand curve of Ionic memorial to John Wood the younger. Leonard nodded, smiled and explained that, although on the map it looked miles away, it was not. When he said so, the man smiled.

CHRISTOPHER LEE 1995

The morning was dull, thick and gloomy, threatening rain, but just before we got into Bath a sun-beam stole across the world and lighted the Queen of the West with the ethereal beauty of a fairy city, while all the land blazed gorgeous with the brilliant and many coloured trees. Almost in a moment the dull dark leaden sky was replaced by a sheet of brilliant blue and the lovely city shone dazzling and lustrous upon the hill sides, her palaces veiled with a tender mist and softened by delicate gleams of pearls and blue.

REV FRANCIS KILVERT 1870-1879

Ye men of Bath, who stately mansions rear
To wait for tenants from Lord knows where,
Would you pursue a plan that cannot fail,
Erect a mad house and enlarge your gaol.

CHRISTOPHER ANSTEY 1724-1805

The City of Bath has so considerably increased in size and the number of inhabitants within the last thirty years, that it is now become one of the most agreeable, as well as the most polite places in the Kingdom; owing chiefly to the elegance of its buildings and the accommodations of strangers, which are superior to any other city in England.

CHRISTOPHER ANSTEY 1802

We dined at half-past four, and stayed to drink tea with my Mother; at seven we returned home in a close carriage, as I do not like to expose myself to the open air. The ground was so slippery the horses could not keep their legs descending the hill to Camerton, but absolutely slid down on their haunches. The servants were gone to bed, and I had much ado to awaken them; it was not nine o'clock, and methinks they might have been found watching.

JOHN SKINNER 1803-1834

◀ *Lansdown Crescent*
The Royal Crescent ▶

I had gradually perused the great Volume of the Author of Nature and was now come to the page which contained a seventh Planet. Had business prevented me that evening, I must have found it the next, and the goodness of my telescope was such that I perceived its visible planetary disc as soon as I looked at it.

WILLIAM HERSCHEL *March 1781*

Farewell then ye streams,
Ye poetical themes!
Sweet fountains for curing the spleen!
I'm griev'd to the heart
Without cash to depart,
And quit this adorable scene!
Where gaming and grace
Each other embrace,
Dissipation and piety meet:
May all, who've a notion
Of cards or devotion,
Make Bath their delightful retreat!

CHRISTOPHER ANSTEY *1766*

*W*ill this find you in the Vale of Ewyas, or have you taken wing for Bath, which, in spite of thirty years' labour toward spoiling it, still remains the pleasantest city in the kingdom? I remember it when it ended at the Crescent, and there was not a house on the Bathwick side of the river. The longest walk in which I was ever indulged was to a cottage—the cottage we called it, in a little orchard, a sweet sequestered spot at that time - my ne plus ultra then, beyond which all was terra incognita. No doubt it is now overgrown with streets. But the only alteration which I cannot forgive is the abominable one converting the South Parade into one side of the square, and thus destroying the finest thing, perhaps the only thing, of its kind in the world. I have often walked upon the terrace by moonlight, after the play, my head full of the heroics which I had been imbibing - and perhaps I am at this day the better for those moonlight walks.

ROBERT SOUTHEY 1799

◀ *Bell Pull*

Reflections ▶

*H*ard by the Pump-room, is a coffee-house for the ladies, but my aunt says, young girls are not admitted, insomuch as the conversation turns upon politics, scandal,philosophy, and other subjects above our capacity; but we are allowed to accompany them to the booksellers' shops, which are charming places of resort; where we read novels, plays, pamphlets and news-papers, for so small a subscription as a crown a quarter; and in these offices of intelligence (as my brother calls them) all the reports of the day, and all the private transactions of the Bath, are first entered and discussed.

TOBIAS SMOLLETT   1766

I do not propose Chaises all the way; I only propose or, implore that you will not, thus weakened, take a place straight to Bath, which, without some rest half way, would almost demolish you, & even exact travelling all night. Do you think of it, I supplicate you. If you could pass a day or two at Bridgewater how much stouter you might arrive at Bath! & what would be that expence compared to Physicians Fees & Apothecaries Drugs?

MADAME D'ARBLAY   1825

It sounds rather strange, but I tell you no lie,
There's many good people that come here to die;
For the London practitioners wisely declare,
When their patients can't breathe, they must try change of air.
Says Sir Walter - "Dear Lady, I thought all the while
That dropsy of yours must proceed from the bile;
The waters of Bath have made wonderful cures
Of many I know, in such cases as yours.
You'll go down directly to Bath if you're wise."
So down goes my Lady directly - and dies -

CAM HOBHOUSE   1811

◀ *Door Knocker*
Corner of Abbey Green ▶

BATH AMERICAN SOCIETY

PRESIDENT:
THE MAYOR OF BATH

CHAIRMAN OF COMMITTEE: AMERICAN CORRESPONDENT:
T. STURGE COTTERELL. J.P.   CEDRIC CHIVERS. J.P.
HON. SECRETARY :   911-913 Atlantic Avenue, Brooklyn, N.Y.
J.S. CARPENTER. 2, Pierrepont Street.   9, Combe Park, Weston, Bath, England.

At a Meeting held at the Guildhall, on June 2nd, 1910, it was resolved to form a Society for the purpose of establishing a means of communication between this City and its twelve namesakes in the United States of America, represented at the Bath Historical Pagaent of 1909.
They are as follows:

Bath: Illinois.	Bath: Ohio.	Bath: North Carolina.
" Maine.	" South Carolina.	" Pennsylvania.
" New York.	" Michigan.	" South Dakota.
" Missouri.	" New Hampshire.	" Kentucky.

FIRSTLY
It was resolve to ask the Governor of each State, the Mayor or local authority, to appoint a correspondent.

SECONDLY
To arrange for an interchange of literature, and to send over Bath publications to be placed in the local libraries.

THIRDLY
To award yearly a prize or a medal to the most proficient scholar selected by the local authority.

FOURTHLY
On a day arranged in June or July of each year distinguished Americans in this country will be invited to attend a Dinner, on which day a Fete or Entertainment will be specially arranged.

FIFTHLY
The Society will also be a medium of affording assistance and information to American Citizens visiting Bath. Also to encourage in every way possible an increase in the number of those visiting this Country.

◀ Claverton Manor

Prior Park ▶

There is money inough spent upon cock-fightinges tenesplayes parkes bankettinges pageantes and playes serving only for a short tyme ye pleasure oft tymes but of privat persones which have no nede of them. But I have not hearde tell that anye riche man hathe spente upon these noble bathes beynge so profitable for the hole comon welth of Englande one grote these twintye yeares.

DR TURNER 1562

"Then why the devil did you come to Bath, which we all know you can't abide, only to be near her? demanded Mr. Ringwood, exasperated. "To be near her? My God, is that what you think? You must be crazy! Nothing would have induced me to have come here, but one circumstance! I made sure I should find her, in some seminary in Queen's Square, and that is all the reason I had for coming to a place I never mean to set foot in again if I live to be a hundred!"

GEORGETTE HEYER 1944

As a place of public resort for Affluence, Gaiety and Affliction, the city of Bath has long been esteemed one of the most distinguished spots in the Kingdom; and is aptly called the "Cradle of Old Age". For in no place can those advanced in life find so many enjoyments as in the social circles with which this city abounds.

THE ORIGINAL BATH GUIDE 1845

The Valley in which it stands, in any Place, extends (hardly) it felt to half a Mile in Breadth; in most Places less; it is very pleasant and fruitful, and therein are hardly ever seen any Pools, Loughs, or Miry Places; for as soon as any inundation is over, the Waters totally drein away with it, which doubtless contributes much to the Salubrity of the Air.

H C CHAPMAN 1631

◀ *Horseshoe Weir*
Pulteney Bridge ▶

To those occasional visitors of Bath, who may be unacquainted with the localities of this elegant City, it may be necessary to state, that the eastern extremity of Great Pulteney-Street- a street the most spacious and magnificent perhaps in the world, certainly unequalled for the respectability and opulence of its inhabitants.

SYDNEY GARDEN PROSPECTUS 1825

In the evening you can walk through the splendid streets of Bath - magnificent streets lined with Georgian houses standing stiff as lackeys behind pillared porticoes; elegant, formal homes. There is the Circus, the Crescent; there is Pulteney Bridge - England's Ponte Vecchio - there are lovely Georgian gateways, and little queer streets round whose corners it seems you just miss the flash of a red-heeled shoe, the twinkle of feet beneath brocade, the sound of a rather naughty little laugh.

H V MORTON 1927

There is one place in Bath, and one only, where I sometimes feel that I am standing in a great centre of the European tradition. It is on the south bank of the river Avon, and it is best reached by walking up the river path beside the sports grounds. One passes then beneath North Parade Bridge, and emerging from its shadowy underside fringed with ivy and ornamented by enigmatic graffiti, one sees suddenly the heart of the city gracefully disposed about its river.

JAN MORRIS 1976

*O*ur road passes through the villages of Bath-easton and
Bathford, ancient dependencies on the monastery of the
neighbouring city, having to the right the river Avon flowing
through rich meadows, and bounded by that belt of hills which
defend the happy vale of Bath from the storms of the south and east.

REV RICHARD WARNER 1801

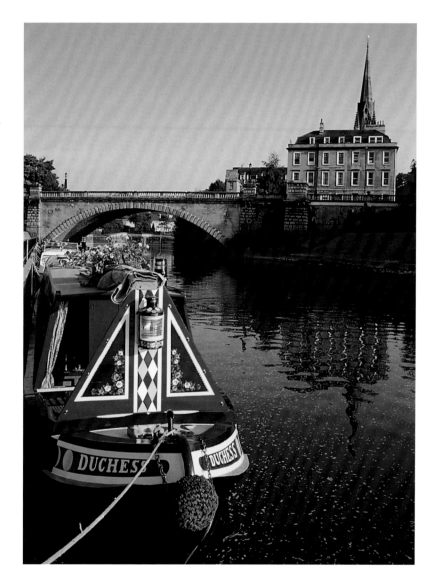

This Kennett and Avon Canal, winding snake like along the side of the hill, gave us wider and wider views as we glided onwards; the last traces of the City began to disappear; far below us the Avon gleamed, a thread of silver between its alders and willows, the heights arose into a series of receding woods along the horizon line....

WILLIAM BLACK 1888

The novelty of the Kennet and Avon Canal, which carried through the Garden and Ride, and compleated in the most handsome manner, with Ornamental Iron Bridges etc. with various Improvements in the Plantations, add considerably to the Picturesque Beauties for which the Spot has been universally admired.

BATH CHRONICLE 1806

◄ *The Kennet and Avon Canal at Bath*

The K & A at Bathampton ►

*T*he toune self of Bradeford stondith on the clining of a slaty rokke, and hath meetely good market ons a weeke. The toune is made al of stone and standith as I cam to it on the hither ripe of Avon.

Ther is a chapelle on the highest place of the toune as I enterid. The fair larg paroche chirch standith bynethe the bridge on Avon ripe. The vicarage is at the west ende of the chirch.

JOHN LELAND

WHEREAS I, ISAAC MILLS,

Gate-Keeper at the Wolly Gate, in the Parish of Bradford, in the County of Wilts, did, on the 20th of October last, strike, beat and abuse, a Servant of Mr. Francis Yerbury, who was coming through the same Gate, with some Sheep of his Master's, notwithstanding he produced a Ticket that he had paid Toll for the same at Staverton Gate; and whereas the said F. Yerbury hath been so kind to put a Stop to a Prosecution that was commenced against me for such an atrocious Offence, I hereby do in this public Manner acknowledge my Fault, and promise never to be guilty of the same again, and am greatly obliged to him on his forgiving me. out of Consideration of the largeness of my Family, paying for this Advertisement, and giving his Man a Trifle for the Injury done him. As witness my Hand the 23 Day of Novemver, 1765

The mark of ISAAC MILLS

That village is, I think, easily the most remarkable and the most beautiful in all Wiltshire. It is beautiful not only by reason of its situation in the meadows beside the river between the eastern and western hills which are not here more than two miles apart, so that Lacock lies in a kind of pass, the pass of the river north and south; but by reason of its noble medieval buildings, and the extensive and splendid remains of the Augustinian convent, the grand old mansion Bewley Court, a glorious church, a great fourteenth century barn, an ancient village cross, and I know not how many fine old houses, indeed the whole place seems full of them, so that altogether Lacock is a place by itself to be beloved for its own sake, to be visited again and again.

EDWARD HUTTON 1919

The pilgrim in search of charm would do well to spend a day in Lacock. It is enchanting. You can stroll down the centuries, lingering in each. In Lacock the keystone of the arch linking present to past is stability. The motto J'y suis, j'y reste might be inscribed above every lintel. It is the England that was. I saw it first in June under the right conditions with nothing to disturb a peace expressing itself as the serenity of a ripe and mellow age. It looked "cared for" and cherished.

HORACE ANNESLEY VACHELL 1933

........This led me to reflect on the inimitable beauty of the pictures of nature's painting which the glass lens of the camera throws upon the paper in its focus - fairy pictures, creations of a moment, and destined as rapidly to fade away. It was probably thus that this idea occurred to me: How charming it would be if it were possible to cause these natural images to imprint themselves durably and remain fixed upon the paper!

........Such is the fact that we may receive on paper the fleeting shadow, arrest it there, and in the space of a single minute fix it there so firmly as to be no more capable of change, even if thrown back into the sunbeam from which it derived its origin.

........When the weather is dark and cloudy, a corresponding allowance is necessary and a greater demand is made upon the patience of the sitter. Groups of figures require no longer time to obtain than single figures would require, since the camera depicts them all at once, however numerous they may be, but at present we cannot well succeed in this branch of art without some previous concern and arrangement. But when a group of persons has been artistically arranged, and trained by a little practice to maintain absolute immobility for a few seconds of a time, very delightful pictures are easily obtained.

WILLIAM HENRY FOX TALBOT 1839

◀ *Oriel Window at Lacock Abbey*
Lacock Abbey Exterior ▶

......a pratie market Town about a mile from Farley Castelle.

LELAND c1540

*S*o rode a very good way led to my great content by our landlord
to Phillip's Norton with great pleasure being now come into
Somerset-shire where my wife and Deb mightily joyed thereat I com-
mending the country as endeed it deserves.
.... at Ph. Norton I walked to the church and there saw an a very
ancient tomb of some K. Templar I think and here saw the tombstone
whereon there were only two heads cut which the story goes were the
and credibly were two sisters call the fair maids of Foscott that had
two bodies upward and one below and there lie buried. Here is also
a fine ring of six bells and chimes mighty tuneable. having dined
very well.(Paid) 10 shillings.

SAMUEL PEPYS 12th June 1668

*I*f the evening be fine and warm, there is nothing better in life
than to lounge before the inn door in the sunset, or lean over the
parapet of the bridge, to watch the weeds and the quick fishes. It is
then, if ever, that you taste Joviality to the full significance of that
audacious word.

ROBERT LOUIS STEVENSON 1850-1894

*A*s soon as you cross the bridge, low-arched and delightfully
buttressed, you begin to ascend the sharp slope of Castle
Combe, with its hanging woods above, a perfect background for the
many-gabled, many-chimneyed, dormer-windowed houses. You can
pause at every step to gladden your eyes. The details of windows,
doors, porches, eaves, and the irregularity of roof-line are absorbing.
The village street is narrow and what the French term "accidente".
Happy chance, not design, determined it's character.

HORACE ANNESLEY VACHELL 1933

I know a village where there are hardly any clocks, where no one
knows more of the days of the week than by a sort of instinct for
the fete on Sundays, and where only one person can tell you the day of
the month, and she is generally wrong.

ROBERT LOUIS STEVENSON 1850-1894

*A*s the sun shone through the roof of beech boughs overhead the very air seemed gold and scarlet and green and crimson in the deep places of the wood and the red leaves shone brilliant standing out against the splendid blue of the sky. A crowd of wood pigeons rose from the green and misty azure hollows of the plantation and flapped swiftly down the glades, the blue light glancing off their clapping wings. I went by the house down to the lakeside and crossed the water by the hatches above the cascade. From the other side of the water the lake shone as blue as the sky and beyond it rose from the water's edge the grand bank of sloping woods glowing with colours, scarlet, gold, orange and crimson and dark green. Two men were fishing on the further shore of an arm of the lake and across the water came the hoarse belling of a buck while a coot fluttered skimming along the surface of the lake with a loud cry and rippling splash.

REV FRANCIS KILVERT

INDEX

This index contains extended captions to the photographs.

like a medieval town until a succession of royal visitors came to bath in the waters. Charles II came in 1677 with his wife Catherine, in the hope that the waters would cure her childless condition. Charles liked Bath and returned on later visits with his mistresses. In 1687 James II came followed by his daughter Princess Anne a few years later. By 1703 Anne had been Queen for a year and visited Bath four times. With all this royal patronage Bath became a fashionable destination for more people. Bath at this time was ill-equipped to cater for visitors.

The "Subscription" system was used to finance the facilities needed by the visitors. Money was raised by selling advance subscriptions or membership. Access to tea rooms, gardens, balls, firework displays, walks, book-shops and churches were paid for by the month or other periods of time. To walk and be seen in one of the gravel walks was a fashionable thing to do. When wet the Pump Room was open for similar perambulations. For Society it was desirable for single ladies to meet men of similar standing. The exclusive nature of the subscription ensured this. Proprietary Chapels sold pew space by the month and needed exciting preachers to bring in the crowds.

At the infancy of this development three crucial men arrived in Bath. All were young and ambitious.

Richard "Beau" Nash arrived in 1705 at the age of 29. A Card-sharp and gambler, he was attracted by the rich pickings from fashionable visitors. When he arrived the City was a shambles. He had an innate sense of order, manners and behaviour which came to the fore when he was made "Master of Ceremonies". In this role he laid down codes of conduct for everyone from the aristocratic visitors to the sedan chairmen. He was instrumental in getting the Pump Room and other facilities built.

Nash had a strong will to "civilise" the City of Bath and make it an attractive place to visit. He disciplined the aristocrats for behaving snobbish with the lower Gentry. To combat drunkenness he introduced restricted hours for drinking which spread throughout the country. His eleven o'clock closing time is still with us today. One measure he took was a stand against dueling. At the time it was common for gentlemen to wear swords at all times. It was part of their dress. Any argument could easily turn into a sword fight. Duels would frequently follow. Nash decided to stamp out dueling by banning the wearing of swords in the City of Bath. Although there were protests, his edict was obeyed. Soon dueling became less frequent and the idea spread to the rest of the Kingdom.

Ralph Allen arrived from Cornwall at the age of 17, in 1712, and two years later became Chief Postmaster. He made a fortune when he took over the rural postal service in England. He later bought the quarries above Bath and made a second fortune supplying stone to the new buildings.

Allen was described by all as a very kind man. Squire Allworthy in Henry Fielding's "Tom Jones" was modelled on Ralph Allen who fed the author at Prior Park while he wrote the novel. The description of the Squire in the book describes Allworthy/Allen as a man who had raised a large fortune with the most perfect preservation of his integrity and without the least injustice or injury to any other person.

John Wood, the architect, arrived at the age of 22 in 1727. He had earlier sent detailed and extensive plans for the development of Bath to Ralph Allen. Wood was keen on the "Palladian" style of architecture. His plans did not meet with much approval by the Corporation of the day but the identity of Georgian Bath was created by him.

After several improvements to the existing buildings and facilities John Wood started on his grand plan. As an architect he designed the facades of his buildings and acted as an entrepreneur to get them built. Each house was financed and built separately within his basic plan. In this way grand squares and terraces were created without the need for one person to finance them all. Wood left the interior details to the local builders and their clients which meant that each house had a different floor plan. He controlled the external details.

A local entrepreneur, Thomas Harrison, built an Assembly Room in 1708. It was financed on the subscription principle as were Harrison's Gardens next door. It became the social hub of Bath. With such a money making example other buildings followed suit. In truth they were little more than gaming rooms but their exclusive nature ensured the patronage of well-bred visitors.

Throughout its heyday Bath was changing fast. New buildings were under construction almost continuously. What with the noise, dust, horse manure and beggars it would probably be considered a bit of a dump by present day standards. The one saving grace, which created its prosperity; it was the most fashionable place in the country. When the Regency era made sea bathing popular, the smart set moved to Brighton. Bath slowly turned into an ordinary, but still elegant, country town.

48 BRICKED UP WINDOW
In 1696 Parliament introduced a Window Tax. This was to pay for the cost of re-minting damaged coins. In 1792 houses having seven to nine windows were taxed 2 shillings. Ten to nineteen windows cost 4 shillings. Windows were bricked up to reduce the tax burden. This window near Pulteney Bridge has an amusing Trompe l'oeil painting.

49 QUEEN SQUARE
Begun in 1729 this was John Wood's first planned development.

50 THE ROYAL CRESCENT
Built by John Wood, The Younger between 1767 and 1775 this is the pre-eminent building in Bath.

51 1, THE CRESCENT
Beautifully kept by The Bath Preservation Trust this house has a true feel for the elegance of the period.

52 & 53 VICTORIA GARDENS

54 LANSDOWN CRESCENT
John Palmer designed this crescent with its fine views and built it between 1780 and 1793. It fits well into its situation and is characteristic of the theoretic views on landscape current at the time. It still looks good today.

55 THE ROYAL CRESCENT AT NIGHT

56 & 57 THE CIRCUS
The great dream of John Wood to create a roman style circus was started in 1754. He died three months after work started and it was left to his son to finish the grand design.

58 BELL PULL

59 REFLECTIONS
Architects followed the Palladian ideas of John Wood into this century. This 1930's Post Office fits into the pattern and texture of Georgian Bath.

60 DOOR KNOCKER

61 ABBEY GREEN CORNER

62 & 63 CLAVERTON MANOR
Sir Jeffry Wyatville designed this handsome house in 1820. It is now the site of the excellent American Museum. (It is also the site of one of my earliest photographic assignments, over 30 years ago). Many of the rooms are decorated in particular american styles and periods.

64 to 70 PULTENEY BRIDGE
Sir William Pulteney owned the Bathwick Estate, on the opposite side of the river to the City. While developments were pushing ever onward on the other side of the city his plans would not be profitable until there was a

bridge across the river. Robart Adam, an architect famous for the neo-classical Palladian style, was commissioned to design the road bridge. Started in 1769, it took five years to build.

71 RIVER AVON AT BATH

72 & 73 RIVER AVON & NARROW-BOAT

The river at Bath has always been an efficient means of communication and transport to Bristol and the sea. When the Kennet and Avon Canal was built narrowboats left the canal at Bath and continued to Bristol on the river. The industrial use of the waterway has now finished. Replica and re-built narrowboats are used for leisure cruising.

74 KENNET AND AVON CANAL

In 1788, at the height of "Canal Mania" it was decided to link the River Avon with the River Thames by canal. This would create a cross country transport route for coal, building materials and other goods. John Rennie, the engineer was to complete the task in 1810. Although the canal was very successful it fell into decline and disuse when the railways offered greater flexibility and faster transport. The Kennet and Avon Canal Trust have re-opened the waterway in recent times. It is now possible to reach London from Bath by inland waterway once again.

75 BATHAMPTON CANAL

Just outside Bath the Kennet and Avon Canal passes through the village of Bathampton.

76 THE RIVER AVON

The river at Bradford-on-Avon flows through an attractive valley of fields and water meadows towards Bath.

77 BRADFORD ON AVON

Many of the villages involved in the wool trade employed small scale home-looms. In Bradford-on-Avon the strong flow of water in the River Avon allowed bigger water-mills which encouraged the growth of cloth factories. As early capitalists the factory owners built fine houses which reflect the prosperity of the town.

The ancient bridge has a small lockup or "chapel". Usually it was drunks who cooled off in the tiny cell. John Wesley, the teetotal Methodist preacher, is rumoured to have been locked up here.

78 - 81 LACOCK

Lacock was owned at the time of the Doomsday Book by Edward of Salisbury. He was the son of one of William the Conquerors invading knights. His great-grandaughter Ela, The Countess of Salisbury, founded the Abbey in 1232 in memory of her husband. Her husband was William Longespee, the illegitimate son of Henry II. She had good royal connections to endow the Abbey. Oaks from Royal forests were given for its construction. Land and licences were given to grant the Abbey with an income. The Abbey was a nunnery for well bred ladies.

The village was owned by the Abbey and most of the tenants paid their rent in tithes. This is a type of barter economy where the villagers would pay according to what they produced, barley, wool, thatching straw, etc.. There is a fine Tithe Barn in the centre of the village where these were stored. Those without land provided services in exchange for their rent.

The village prospered with the wool industry. Houses in the village were re-built to accommodate larger looms. Lacock enjoyed considerable stability until the Reformation.

The Abbey was closed by Henry VIII in 1539 and sold to Sir William Sharington for £783. Sir William proceeded to convert the Abbey for domestic use making various changes. The heirless Sir William left the Abbey, and most of the village, to his brother Sir Henry Sharington whose daughter, Olive, married Sir John Talbot.

Upheavals during the Civil War resulted in a fine of £1,100 when the house surrendered to the Parliamentary forces. In later years Talbots were to enter parliament as MPs, including William Henry Fox Talbot in 1832.

William Henry Fox Talbot's name will forever be associated with his invention of the negative/positive process in photography. He was an enthusiastic scientist and inventor. He dabbled in many different fields including electro-magnatism and electric energy. He was a friend of John Herschel and Josiah and Thomas Wedgwood. All of them had been experimenting with preserving the image produced by the Camera Obscura.

In 1839 a few months before Fox Talbot announced his invention, the frenchman, Louis Daguerre announced the invention of the Daguerreotype. Although daguerreotypes were used commercially, with great success, for several years, it was not the route that photography

would follow. The negative/positive process was patented as the Calotype by Fox Talbot.

When Sir John Herschel saw Fox Talbot's published results he immediately duplicated them and, at the same time, suggested the name "photography" for the new process. Daguerre gave his invention to the French nation in return for a pension, but retained the patent in Britain. The French thought that by allowing free use to the process further developments would happen sooner. Fox Talbot zealously guarded the patent of his Calotype process which instead of stifling research encouraged inventors to improve and thereby circumvent the patents.

William Henry Fox Talbot has a rightful place as the "father of photography", without which this book would not exist.

80 & 81 ORIEL WINDOW, LACOCK ABBEY

This window is the subject of the earliest known photograph, made by Fox Talbot. The diamond leading of the windows can still be seen in the original photograph.

Lacock Abbey and Lacock Village are now owned by the National Trust and have been perfectly preserved. To visit Lacock is to step back in time.

82 & 83 NORTON ST PHILIP

The George Inn at Norton St. Philip is generally agreed to be the oldest in the country. Once part of a monastery it is also one of the most interesting buildings from the period.

84 - 87 CASTLE COMBE
A Brief History

The Fosse Way, a Roman road, which runs north to south across England passes close to the top of the valley. The Romans built a fort on a spur overlooking the valley, or combe, below.

After the Romans left the Saxons occupied the site. During the Saxon era the castle was used for protection from the marauding bands of Danish invaders, who were based in Chippenham. A battle in the next-door parish of Slaughterford ended the Danish occupation of the area.

After this battle the middle ages were largely peaceful and the village started to develop.

Seventy years after the Norman conquest a new castle was built on the same site as the roman fort. The barony of the Dunstanville family soon had control over several other parts of the county. Castle Combe prospered and enjoyed relative stability with their own courts, licensing and law enforcement systems. Butchers were reprimanded for gambling in their shops. Ale was brewed by the church and the publicans on a rota basis. The village was self-sufficient producing woolen cloth for trade while the valley farmers grew food and reared sheep.

However, the absentee baron, Sir Bartholomew de Badlesmere became involved in anti-royalist protests. Edward II sentenced him to be; "Drawn for his treason, hanged for his robberies, and beheaded for his flight. Inasmuch as he was the King's seneschal his head should be spiked on the gate at Canterbury." All this happened in 1322.

With no one left to claim the castle the villagers began taking the stone down the hill to re-cycle into new houses in the combe. The weaving of wool became the main industry in Castle Combe which was becoming a small town.

The reason why places like Castle Combe, (and Lacock), became centres of cloth production is fascinating. The increased urbanization of towns such as Bath, Bristol, Wells and Salisbury took people from self-sufficient farming into a trading economy. The sparsely populated moorlands of Devon and Cornwall were perfect for rearing sheep but there was no market for the meat or the wool in remote country areas. The sheep were herded hundreds of miles across the country by drovers on special drovers roads. After the animals were slaughtered for meat there was a need for an industry to process the hides and wool. With so much weaving in the west country, technical advances made these towns pre-eminent in the trade.

Sir John Fastoff was responsible for introducing some of the technical improvements to Castle Combe. He invested new money into what had become a very busy little town. Shakespeare may have based Sir John Falstaff on him. It is believed that "blankets" were invented in Castle Combe by a weaver called Blankett. The mists and damp in the village made it very cold at night.

Unfortunately the By Brook which powered the essential water wheels for processing the fibres became a trickle and the weaving industry in the town collapsed. As houses became derelict the town eventually became a small agricultural village.

Castle Combe is generally considered to be the prettiest village in England. Whereas some of the other villages prettify themselves in a rather artificial way Castle Combe has a natural beauty. It has two big advantages. Firstly, the village is in an exceptionally pretty spot and built mostly in one period from local materials. Secondly, it was used as a film location in 1966 for the film Dr. Dolittle. The film crew did a certain amount of "tidying" for the film. The villagers liked what the film people did and have almost kept it that way ever since!

The village is not preserved by any official body like the National Trust. It is the way it is because the residents like it that way.

88 HOLLYHOCKS
Typical English flowers against a Bath stone wall.

89 MISTY MORNING
Dawn in the Avon valley.

THE WRITERS

CHRISTOPHER ANSTEY
MADAM D'ARBLAY
JANE AUSTEN
M J B BADDELEY
BANWELL
MAX BEERBOHM
JOHN BETJEMAN
WILLIAM BLACK
JAMES BOSWELL
VICTOR CANNING
H C CHAPMAN
CHARLES DICKENS
MARGARET DODS
JOHN EVELYN
SAMUEL GALE
HENRY HARRINGTON
THOMAS HARDY
WILLIAM HERSCHEL
GEORGETTE HEYER
CAM HOBHOUSE
W H HUDSON
HENRY OF HUNTINGTON
EDWARD HUTTON
MIRZA ABUL HASSAN KHAN

REV FRANCIS KILVERT
CHRISTOPHER LEE
JOHN LELAND
LORD LYTTON
LYDIA MELFORD
ISAAC MILLS
H V MORTON
JAN MORRIS
SAMUEL PEPYS
RICHARD BRINSLEY SHERIDAN
LOUIS SIMON
JOHN SKINNER
TOBIAS SMOLLETT
ROBERT SOUTHEY
ROBERT LOUIS STEVENSON
LYTTON STRACHEY
ALGERNON CHARLES SWIN-BURNE
CORNELIUS TACITUS
WILLIAM HENRY FOX TALBOT
DR TURNER
HORACE ANNESLEY VACHELL
REV RICHARD WARNER
JOHN WOOD

ATMOSPHERE also publish other books of Bob Croxford's
photographs in the same general format

All the books can be ordered at any good bookshop.
In case of difficulty phone 01326 240180 or
email books@atmosphere.co.uk

FROM CORNWALL WITH LOVE	*ISBN 09521850 0 8*
FROM DEVON WITH LOVE	*ISBN 09521850 1 6*
FROM DORSET WITH LOVE	*ISBN 09521850 3 2*
FROM THE COTSWOLDS WITH LOVE	*ISBN 09521850 4 8*
HAMPSHIRE	*ISBN 09521850 5 9*
A VIEW OF AVALON	*ISBN 09521850 6 7*
THE CORNISH COAST (115 x 165 size)	*ISBN 09521850 7 5*

ACKNOWLEDGEMENTS

Many thanks to Stella Pierce for her research work on the anthology.

Thanks to Julie and Karen for invaluable help on this book.
Thanks to The Bath Preservation Trust for kindly allowing me to photograph inside NUMBER 1, ROYAL CRESCENT. The photograph on page 51 remains their copyright.
Thanks to The National Trust for allowing the use of the photographs taken at Lacock Abbey.
Ryker Jeal built the wall on the cover using stone carved by G Williams & Sons Ltd of Bath.

No compiler or researcher of anthologies can work without the efforts of previous researchers. Credit is due to David Gadd for his book GEORGIAN SUMMER and Christopher Pound for his book GENIUS OF BATH.

The quotations from EVERYMAN'S ENGLAND by Victor Canning are reproduced with permission of Curtis Brown Group Ltd, London on behalf of the Estate of Victor Canning. Copyright Victor Canning
The quotation from THE BATH DETECTIVE by Christopher Lee published by Sinclair-Stevenson is reproduced with kind permission of The Random House Group Ltd..
The quotations from IN SEARCH OF ENGLAND by H V Morton are reproduced with permission of
Methuen Publishing Ltd. Copyright cMarion Wasdell and Brian de Villiers.
The poem THE NEWEST BATH GUIDE by John Betjeman is reproduced by kind permission of John Murray (Publishers) Ltd.
The quotation from A PERSIAN KING AT THE COURT OF KING GEORGE 1809-10 by Mirza Abul Hassan Khan edited and translated by Margaret Morris Cloake
published by Barrie & Jenkins Publishers is reproduced with kind permission of The Random House Group Ltd.
The quotation from TRAVELS by Jan Morris is reproduced with kind permission of A P Watt Ltd on behalf of Jan Morris.
The quotations from FRIDAY'S CHILD by Georgette Heyer c1946 are reproduced with kind permission of Sir Richard Rougier

Every effort has been made to contact all the copyright holders. Should the publishers have made any mistakes in attribution we will be pleased to make the necessary arrangements at the first opportunity.